AF479568

This book is dedicated to all the future leaders of this world. To my loving wife T'aira and our amazing children Kennedy, Micah, Joshua and in loving memory of TimmyEvan, Spirit & Sovereign.

Made ready for publication by All God Everything, LLC
Author and creative expression produced by:
Maurice I Jones, Micah Jones & Joshua Jones
ISBN: 9798841143079

# How can
# I lead?

# What is a leader?

# Can I be a leader?

# YES!

# I can be

# a leader!

ELORE

# YOU
## can be a
## leader too !

# I CAN LEAD
## by playing
## nice with
## others.

# I CAN LEAD by learning new things.

I Can Read
Biscuit's
New Trick

I CAN LEAD
by helping
others to
read.

# I CAN LEAD
## by teaching
## others how
## to draw.

# I CAN LEAD

# by helping

# others in

# need.

# I CAN LEAD by making others smile.

# I CAN LEAD by loving others when they are sad.

# I CAN LEAD by going to bed on time.

In all that
you do,
you can be a
leader too!

# Please Check Out these other books available on Amazon.com

# ORDER THEM ALL NOW!